LIFE AS *IT*

LIFE AS *IT*

Poems

Daneen Wardrop

 THE ASHLAND POETRY PRESS

Printed in the United States of America

ISBN: 978-0-912592-90-9

LCCN: 2016951828

Cover art: Mary Bauermeister, *Four Cubed Variations*, 1968, mixed media lens box, 11"x11"x7" courtesy of the artist and The Pavel Zoubok Gallery.

Cover design: Nicholas Fedorchak

Author photo: Patricia Pettinga

Acknowledgments & Notes

For including the poems that have become this volume I am immensely grateful to the editors and staffs of the following publications:

AGNI, Barrow Street, Blackbird, Blue Mesa Review, Denver Quarterly, Ecotone, FIELD, Pinstripe Fedora, Poetry in Michigan / Michigan in Poetry, The Seattle Review, The Southern Review, Sycamore Review

I am indebted to David St. John for selecting this manuscript. I'm thankful for the inspiration and camaraderie provided by Nancy Eimers, Bill Olsen, Lesley Amolsch, Katherine Joslin, Tom Bailey, Hedy Habra, the Kalamazoo Cousin moms and daughters, the breakfast group, the Friends group, my colleagues, and my loving family.

Contents

III. Caesura

IV. Nth

V. Form

VI. Ways

I.

UNNUMBERED

Track

Heated and flushed after a vision, St. Teresa asked a sister nun if she would cut her hair. When cut, Teresa's hair let off such lush fragrance the sister cherished it for relic, kept the sweet hank to track inspiration. Paul McCartney was inspired by Roy Orbison's "Pretty Woman," guitar riffing in the grooves of "Day Tripper." Listen: they circle each other, *the kind I'd like to meet*, and the thing that *took me so long*. Feel it in the sweat, mid-song, thrown off a Beatle head. *I order you not to think such nonsense*, St. Teresa told the sister, and *throw that thing out with the trash*. Or open the song to find a place so precisely contoured you can walk through it only with syncopated stride.

A Race

My daughter LiLi and her friend have collected slugs to set up a race in the driveway. We may want to ask questions that are about bright, lapsing ribbons instead of last things. When still a teenager, St. Teresa, seriously ill, fell into a coma and woke three days later during her own funeral rites, wax already poured to seal her eyes, family wringing memory as their tears dampened her face. I'm startled in moments of darkest July to find I'm held to the world by the ravel of a guitar riff, trill of a cardinal. Teresa gave the slip to the under life, came back on a thread. Some minutes ago the girls abandoned the race, now slid to silver by fraction, by fraction, gaining the shade.

Third

In the Arctic, explorers sometimes feel there is one person more than the headcount. My good friend, decades ago, wandering rainbows, wondered, Where's the other one of us?—and he knew there was one who stayed there just to the side of our prismic eyes. I only know about Arctic explorers from Eliot's waste: *Who is the third who walks always beside you?* Snow falls on the third person. Star-confetti. In the front yard, there's a three-day-old snowwoman doing her melted yoga. Hold: tree-pose, warrior pose, down-dog. The snow in her blurs, less and less her, almost headless now.

Life as *It*

They say Buddha called many animals to him but not the cat. Surely the story is lax on this one. Surely no one was watching on this one. After looking a while at an upward spill of incense smoke the cat disappeared along a mouse-flicking path. Some Buddhists say it's important for the breath to wander in the belly. When I see a palette's paint wet and deep with colors I want to kiss it. How complex what passes for ready. The breath can do what it wants. Dragons roast meatloaves with their breaths, oxen hump in the fields, snakes unfinish circles. The cat walks through grassblades strumming.

At a Time

LiLi says she can tell the notes in her stomach when she plays flute, feel the melody from inside. St. Teresa claimed at first she could see God's face only feature by feature because seeing the whole at once would undo her. "You play flute," Li tells me, "and you *want* to play flute." Mostly she wants to fit the silver pieces—they're real silver—together, while her pet slug, Eliza, lounges in an open sour cream carton in the deck's shade. I could take seeing one feature at a time. Teresa said her bones disjoined. I want to see a creature through grains of the earth. A slug, it turns out, has a cute profile, various to the horns' extrusions and retractions.

Pick

LiLi and her babysitter saw a turtle laying eggs in a light rain and held their umbrella over her. Sun would have dripped through the wet as the turtle went about her work, tranced, not needing the umbrella. Today, at the sale table, I pick up a book on Zen. Next week they will revisit the turtle birthsite, babies hatched and gone, bring me back an abandoned curl of shell, part malleable, part hardened to brisk, and I'll keep it for treasure. I open the half-off book and land on a chapter, "Have No Preferences." I close the book and leave it—alas, my preference. There's a short half-shelf life for the thing that might half-happen to you. Those turtles know what to do. I wish I was gentler.

Unnumbered

In some states of ecstasy, Teresa found she was both a *me* and a *her* together in the same rough dress, the same smooth hour. She heard birdcall clear and cut as silhouette. Our good friends found a saint buried in their lawn, hauled her out, dirt crusted in wooden eye cavities and ear hollows. The wooden gown swelled with a faint color, rose paint in the swaths. These are other people's lives, I may be intruding into their stories but love the blur, like Teresa's hearing later in life: *the rushing of unnumbered birds.*

Untitled

As LiLi falls asleep I sit crosslegged at her bed's end, sink into the unknowing that mixes around the edges of finger knuckle, belly crux, shoulder trajectory. From Suzhou, China, city of gardens, I have carried her on my back, brought her to this evening and what it evens out, like the city of Suzhou floats on the Yangtze. Whatever unknowing invites, whatever it keeps at bay, sees through me, lavender to lavender, I fold, transparent, into it. Dusk may trim dolls to look like cups, may sit down next to me, launch a new moon like a leveling bubble. Though she may turn the unloosed body into yawn, I fold. Though she may swim the width of the trundle bed into the unknowing, I fold. into the. unknowing I. fold into.

Forehead

So I can lean my forehead against St. Teresa's and feel her thought coming to rhythm. Some facts you can't come back from: a spider has 48 knees. In a subtropical place during a storm once, I watched a fist-sized spider struggle and mince along a strand from the house to the woods. Of the pelting rain, the strand was firmer colored. I don't think it was a matter of belief. The place was my parents'. Teresa's hand the gestures, the supernumerary things rain can count on. Her head would close over mine and I would spin.

II.

ASK

Fit

My name is Happenstance-Door. His is I-Know. Because of the brocaded light entry, because moths fidget at the porchlight. Or because I'm afraid of my past, show me someone who isn't. It's a random door that throws itself wide for him to amble in, anonymous to himself. Slowly our names turn into individual letters. Buddha says, *All component things in the world are changeable.* When I was away on a trip he rehinged that door, and I thought it had somehow unsqueaked itself. Component things can fling themselves into the many ways. "Things don't fix themselves," he said with a tilted smile apart from his face. Even though whatever is replete is about to be jiggled and repleted again. As betweenness seems forever to urge us.

Model

Off the top of my head I'd have to say it was the fact that he was chosen to be Joseph by the artist down the street. She needed a model, liked his brown lips, welled eyes that might register pigeons in the rafters. This happened about the same time someone stole the baby Jesus from the crèche in the downtown park. Which bears no relation, except that it says something about the ways of nonrelation in Kalamazoo. That summer, a few miles west of town, we found a memorial park a farmer had crafted: dozens of wind sculptures made from orange and pink plastic plates. I don't know what's memorialized. The plates are beautiful in variegated sun. Settled in back of a country convenience store, the park bears the exact degree of nonrelationship to the man who modeled for Joseph as he does to my living room. He lived with me two years, made us pizza on Thursdays.

Ask

In *The Ecstasy of St. Teresa* her toes curl, marble torched from inside. I'm remembering this from scratch: her uncreated lips. As I listen to Hendrix's *Little Wing*, guitar-ravened, Teresa sits in the lap of God, holding music in her mouth: the *ah* of *asleep*, *aloft*, *astonished*, bending moments. *Well, she's walking through the clouds*: a premonitory thing, the body, each finger's lovely spasm. And who can keep away from that summer? Would it be too much this year to ask for two Augusts, given that Teresa's lids remain not altogether open, creping with ecstasy? But I'll never learn a thousand-thousandth of Hendrix's riffs, *fly on*, his fingers longer than easy, and not asking, maybe the point of it.

From a Place Other than the Lake

Where it meets: the coming together of surface: lakeskin. I see this just a little in the gather to the side of his mouth. Air made by the overhead fan tries to drive suburbia out from a bowl of fruit, and we're restless. If the world were altogether black and white, I could give him a strawberry and he would still know its color. We wish we could drive to Lake Michigan today. Here on the table is a nectarine, tie-dyed orange and yellow. It might work instead of beach wind? It lapses for bite? I hold it for him, sure as place is a fineness in desire.

Duet

When we play Clapton's *Wonderful Tonight* he sings, voice fathoming, *And then she asks me, 'Do you feel all right?' And I say yes* . . . I could bend that guitar string all night. Sometimes he sings the song directly to me, though we're on stage and I know it's for show. I add slices of harmony to his chin. Teresa could spontaneously lift, her feet rising inches off the floor. Buddha could multiply his image in all directions. We keep singing, and he shows many faces, brow smoothing with mildness, eyes browning. I have to admit that I like my guitar part better than my harmony. We each caress an involute instrument as if at any moment Teresa will release from her chest birds beating their wings in place. As if at any moment Buddha will use his multiple selves to look into this.

Peripatetic

The sun is on. Peripatetic lovers in their unremitted walking wander into an alley. It's their private confidence that his arm nestling her back lets go an uncharted fragrance, resinous, hint of lemongrass, quick to aspirate. The sun turns down. They duck into a vinyl shop where John Mayer's "Gravity" plays from the outside speakers. The body's a gorge of motion. The lovers will ditch us. My surmise could be a partial surmise. Someone hollers and hollers in the all-too-willing-to-echo alleyway.

Re:

A *Better Homes and Gardens* living room could try to square to mine, resettle in the lamps and vases. But good luck, the room's corners are dotted with stares. The bouquet never speaks to flashes! The flowers would recall themselves: in mirrors live the ones who grow ambient. He patches the porch ceiling, his face working into evening as bats, outside, swing by like toys. Come morning they'll have refolded, *qigong* postures. Re: mirror. Even if we find the right person. Re: one curve of his back upended to first natural light, another curve clean-gone. Re: a skirt of petals around the bottom of the vase.

Walk

At an intersection in Three Rivers, we stand where a bridge arches over a garbled stream on one side of us, an antique shop settles on the other. Is there a way we'd like to go? Quick, name the 10,000 things you love, do it before the *WALK* sign reappears. All the stops on Buddha's bamboo flute might be tuned to the same note so he need not choose intervals, and he'd play a suffusing melody, a tune with its own flexions, risings. The shop's window displays a dovecote for homing pigeons that once lodged on top of a department store. There was a clutching on all floors, coos for a roof. Though we feel our own flexions, as if there were desire in many thighs, the white-lit walker at the intersection light doesn't stroll yet. Perhaps we'll say something later about the loosed birds. We don't need to decide which way.

III.

CAESURA

If Never the Why then at Least the How

This dawn, if a stranger stands outside our house, the panes will glow as stamps, *par avion*. Windows may settle by noon, but now they wish for sex straight out of sleep. A cupola of wild geese launches a mansion. He sleeps turned from me, pang of light on his forehead. Too jealous for coherence, we spoke last night in interjections, every tooled puncture of his belt slid past what I can't accept from a silver morning, as a hand finds aqua lines tense at the back of a knee. Then, what I can accept. The amazing thing about skin, that it's continuous.

Caesura

Come in come in—

on your knees,

the stark openings

you come—

toppling shoulders,

The parable for

the corner of your mouth

I'm stuck here,

If I were doing

loving you

always eraser crumbs

hesitating around

of tulips by the porch

your partly erased jeans,

and hair the color of shine.

the corner of your mouth is

a year from now.

my head flat as a sheet.

my job right,

would be redundant.

Caesura

Toast, applebutter,

on the CD player,

over the plate,

tweak   fillip   patter

but lumbering in relation to

the space between—

the saints

what flight

forestall? Many-hued

Anxiety's moth

was last night.

Dave Matthews

your shoulders hunched

you and I watch finches

faster than we can think,

how we can feel—

I imagine

ate butterflies for breakfast—

would they foretell,

wings around us.

at the porchlight

Tonight there'll be two.

Third

If I could live on a note it would be *mi*. As it forms a two-tone chord with the note, *do*. If the house could live on a note it would be: a melody releases itself into his redbrown hair. Even when dogs sob somewhere in the background or leaf confetti blows sideways like a storm. *The important thing is not to think much but to love much*, says Teresa, who could levitate with love at any unexpected moment. He and I find third and fifth harmonies with the sparrows stringing past us, intervals thrown into confused tufts of grass. At times Teresa directed other nuns to sit on her to keep her from floating away.

Caesura

Morning gaze

light flutes your chin

in the window, your dog

furrows on puddle surfaces—

As you lay in sleep—

even bones—

more trusting than confused,

at a provisional tilt

angling his neck, turns, spreads

This isn't whimsy—

everything has pitch,

more beat than solid—

Field Devoid of Fate

Absolute and leeched white: slab of sky between day and evening. Maples perch. Doesn't the scene need a person walking down the sidewalk to retain itself? Squirrels run dispatch across wires, vines lace and unlace trellises. Yu from Hunan came upon the Temple of Crows, stepped inside the room filled with a crow mural, crow's eyes the saturated tips of ink brushes. My porch stairs descend into evening like steps into a swimming pool. Yu appeared to his crow wife of the teeming eyes: in black robes, they flew together into the mural. A young couple, evening-textured, amble down my street. Next to my house, at the end of a chain, a three-legged dog sits at the ready. The maples, themselves almost extinguished, condone and gentle this.

Caesura

So if the street is stubbed   with snow, so if bread yelps

from the toaster,   so if the body is open

to parting— I anticipate   as a bird feeder,

arms flat out—   Perhaps erasers cannot work

on outstretched things.   With your long fingers once,

you erased   a lawnmower, sugar bowl, denim shirt.

Did it, easy,   all in one morning—

Transverberation

Exhumed, Teresa's body was found to have a punctured heart, just as she'd written it would. *Transverberation* they call it, a striking through of glory into flesh. The barefoot saint walks through the many ways of ardor, predicates reverberation, when arms crimp breasts, hands fondle wrists, fingers pet naked feet blistered and shining. And of course, when a spear thrusts into a heart. As I sit up in bed I have the sensation that my eyelids move at a different pace from the rest of my face. Plaster sifts behind these walls, the corners want to tryst. He put up these curtain brackets, the window showing more sky than it can possibly use. We're all shoeless.

IV.

NTH

Blue Jay and Something Else

The blue jay's all false sky, stays prinked on the branch, stuck announcement that the sky is happening. Then it lays for the cat. I steep oolong as his hand dips at the neck of a Gibson acoustic, tune distracted by a couple notes left in the sound hole. A dropped pick still lodges in there. The cat's whiskers resonate with watching. Blameless cat: neither sharp nor flat, her bristles tremble with thrill. Until the sky needs a lesson for the umpteenth time, and the jay throws itself into the real. And how the sky must feel, how the tip of that wing's feather. And how the whiskers must track it.

Nth

November is the Norway of the year. And fjords are my eyes, an ordinal seeing all over. That's a lot of seeing. The clumpy things on the deck—clay pot?—a child's chair?—clogs?—whatever they were, flattening to powder now. I have North-Sea-waves for a mouth. My heart, still as a cut circle of felt, is one bit of nth. Like the fact of many blossoms, there is a look impossible to practice. There is a look much like the coming-on of momentum—

The sentence, *November is the Norway of the year*, is from Emily Dickinson.

Slide

One must limit the intake of news or go diffuse with takeout, outsource, make-out, outing, fanning out into the corners of November. And the body, a lace of veins, loses count. And the snow after all is one-thousand-thousand wicks. That's the cold's best offer. At just this flick I know it snows, it snows, my accumulated heart. You might put that on a patient's chart. I slide the door open and the body, a tissue of intent, pushes off from a warm deck.

Lie

I've read that aphasics watching a presidential debate laugh at every lie, like snow reads a landscape. It's a watcher's game, laughter is foil crinkling. Must I give up even my small bit of talk? (I admit it is me, despicable truth of elegies, whom I miss). Sometimes snow finishes the punchline, I suppose our bones sparkle inside like that. A friend once told me my mother's stubbornness kept her alive, told me into her stethoscope. Meticulous sparks move by standing still in the storm, they look like *tell me again*. They look like *tell me again, just a little at a time*.

Why Body

Why body inscribed onto space in *this* exact form? It's possible a person's feet are candles. Windows snow. Decks dangle numerable spotlights, the glitter-mobile sways, and by this time something is flung beyond thanks, where we won't have to remember to keep track. I want to light a match. In May, the flowering pear tree bursts, wearing tiny fleece-caps all over itself.

Something There, Something that Might Be There

The day after Independence Day, a friend and I divide a leftover box of sparklers—they catch, spit stars. Hissings thrown from a thin wand in a bent hand. A third person roams among us. Teresa could talk about love for days. She and other nuns cloistered themselves for talk of nothing else. We all want to know about that. A stray firecracker sounds like bacon fried in an iron skillet tastes. Up the hill, belated home firecrackers stomp bubblewrap on the horizon. She could wait, lucky saint, and Jesus would come at her like a bachelor, sparklers sizzling around a face. In a circle never quite met. The way we all see each other anyway.

V.

FORM

Exchange

The Buddha says I should exchange myself with others. He says if I ride a mountain bike to tallness, I may disclose the smiley fall. Never mind the stones. Once I saw a drunk guy at a party playing guitar with a steak knife for a pick. Gouge, beat, gouge: he wasn't kidding, little shavings clinging to the pick guard. Should I exchange myself with him, perhaps—prepare a seen for the overthrow of overthrowing?—follow that throb and knack. The nature of suchness: Yes. I strum. Buddha will rent no breeze, spill no secrets to the weather, spread a deep orange coat to catch fear and falling, and shake it out. Prayer beads for eyes. Eyes for tuning.

A Train Goes by during Jam Night at Kraftbrau Pub

The Cyclops headlight debuts. The thing arrives just ten feet outside the pub wall, so massive the air must turn steel to support its shrieking whistle, a C# chord—actually, C# diminished 7th, I think, flanging. And though I can't become the train's metal, I can be the sluice of air between cars, slice, slice, slice. Even though it's night and I can't see it, I can hear where I might fit, the only places I might fit, though inside I'm singing "Gone Gone Gone" with the bluegrass musicians, and it's in D—what those bluegrass guys love to play, in D and fast, and it doesn't matter. When it goes by the lights shake, the dobros and mandolins subsumed into that C# diminished 7th chord. At home sometimes he nods past the cats and me in the kitchen, slice, slice. The 10:09 leaves in its aftermath a wrecked song, keening in slim branches behind the empty lot in the exact same semitones.

Tumble

He and I tumble to *what shall we do*. Sit on the deck, see a swallow, window-shunted, drop into view. We try to hearten ourselves with consolation, it's one kind of invitation, and after long minutes the bird flies away, we're enjoined to simplify. Neighbor's cat in the bushes. In the evening when grasses steam and pines deepen we take it as a sign that one of us can become the other. We don't see the cat. The cat sees us but doesn't have to look. She understands object permanence.

Goose

My friend on his goose farm in Mecosta says the way to walk is around the gooses. Their hisses hurt. And there's goop we might step on. Who would volunteer to walk in such perfection, where poised, always, is the goo down the track? From Buddha's flute the world is born in all its silly ledges. The little goose has prize feather down, the big one a gilded beak like an ancient candle snuffer. In any given moment, maybe only once, maybe only in the center of a lifetime, one chooses to receive everything. Probably the one is an animal. Throw grain at a green tractor, the geese part for us. One aims at my knee.

Turkeyville

In Turkeyville, my friend and I stay for twelve hours to have a slipped belt fixed. I'm sorry, but I can't trust in fate, it feels like a turkey farm. There's not much to do in Turkeyville except eat French fries and reread long, long menus. If I had to trust in fate, I might trust a thread from the hem of a saint, nothing flashy—a mottled brown or gray. Out the restaurant window in brown clouds swings a blinking intersection light, also brown. He and I sit here with melting glasses of iced tea. And I want him to tell me the story again about days and nights of caving, on bellies, gripping the ankles of the person in front of him, with only voices to see each other. I miss him like that, even right in front of me. The traffic light circle turns to lighter brown. We keep on reading. Little marzipan turkeys line up by the cash register.

Form

Back then, I followed the rows and tied cauliflower, dreamed of buying a Marshall amp. Was paid piecemeal. I tied fewer than anyone else, my meal in pieces. We wore thick yellow rubber bands all up and down one arm, grabbed each cauli by the throat, bunched the leaves, pulled a band over its head. If Buddhist form is emptiness, giggling is the question to every passing note. The question may also be just plain hunger. I only made enough money to nail a Marshall logo to my homemade speaker cabinet. If form empties out, it might wreak something incapable of touch. Every day—I mean it—I wanted to steal my roommates' crackers and peanut butter.

Riff

In front of the Sears Tower, amplified by building fronts, air a frisson around the saxophone player: no one cranes to look at rooftop antennae. Sax aureoles rise, trees grow in fonts around the plaza, confetti replicates in purse bottoms, moving against the lining. If lovers were to comb each other's hair with sun it would stay tangled as confetti. A way of the strapless. Lovers' tongues. Hot music a bowl of mixolydian attached to their lips. And no one is saying stop.

Case

Teresa's visions pour until lilacs steam open. In Michigan we have sleighs for veins even when bees mutter, grasshoppers pronk. Cheer up: loneliness is a speck under avalanches. As Teresa herself said, *May God protect me from gloomy saints*. Or: keep trudging. The sun's gambit—to erase memories of snow. I'm grateful for summer's amnesia, for lilacs that turn younger every minute. And we keep a sleeping bag in our trunks, just in case.

Traffic Light

Stopped at the traffic light, Christina Aguilera on the radio: *I am beautiful, no matter what they say*. I turn to the car next to me, windows up, where the driver mouths the same words—to my radio. *Words can't bring me down*—I've read Aguilera had to lie on the floor of the recording studio to sing that song. The car windows seal themselves. But does everyone have a bellybutton? my daughter asked me this morning. Yeah, sure, I wanted to say: everybody has a bellybutton, but some are not magnets. *Trying hard to fill the emptiness*. I've read, though, that Alfred Hitchcock didn't have a bellybutton—maybe because of an operation. And the light's still red, the woman and I continuing to mouth the song. Neither of us talking on a cell phone.

Beethovens

I want at least five Beethovens: the rock-n-roll Beethoven with twisting hair, winch chin, splinters for fingers, a twirling cape of hammers, hammering damnations. When he turns to me the melodic wind off his cape knocks me nonsensical. Does that mean I can't have it? It is bad, my daughter says, to have a mother who never stops singing. From his irascible eyebrows, a head made of rims. If someone asks us, Does it matter if we find the root note of a heartbeat?, we have to answer, Not in the name of enoughness, but of what lets us go. One of the Beethovens conducts a deaf orchestra.

VI.

WAYS

Buddha's Flute

We think we hear it, the velvet melody of lilac. It's played along the nap. Bumblebee interlopers take up residence inside the wooden birdhouse, hanging just a knuckle away when I open the sliding door. A few years ago LiLi splashed orange paint on the birdhouse. Now the bees, topheavy, fly into its flat black disk. A friend of mine used to pet bumbles, tame as cows balancing on grass stalks. That's one smooth itinerary, though in just a moment rain will make it a moot point. Squall's foot to itinerary, unsuited as Buddha's flute is to *isn't*. A pre-teen now, my daughter no longer paints birdhouses, but the bees will stay in there, at least until the rain passes.

Charm

When she was a little girl, Li told me about a friend who asked her mother to sew a half-moon charm into a dress hem. A half-moon neither stays nor goes, curvature finding the precise crook of knee. A curve can do that. With the half moon, Li's friend felt night sky at her calf, even during the day when the horizon is usually so stubborn. Sidewalks don't have to mean, sycamores don't have to lose their piebald bark, not a single passerby's stride has to yield to a sprinkler. Even inside a hem, sparkle buys a certain density of light. LiLi has an owl charm she might want me to hide in a hem. I can place this thought on the windowsill and leave it to lilt or fall as it may. If all things in the world were to come to one curve it would, I think, be casual.

Very

The mnemonic LiLi's teacher gave her for the solar system: Mom Very Enthusiastically Made Jelly Sandwiches Under No Protest. The *Protest* part no longer in play now that *Pluto*'s gone. But the Mom—man, she slaps that bread together chipper as a kindergarten teacher, sun hotter than crayoned red. What's the mnemonic for talking to the principal about kids needing art? Mom. Enthusiastically. For insisting how paint arcs skies and kids burn to splash it there? Very. A renegade planet can happen in a bounce, stars brimming, quick limbs of meteors. And Li and her friends want to eat the sandwiches they press together with bologna and cool-whip. Under No. Protest anything *but* pouring a whole bottle of dishsoap, when I wasn't looking, onto the Slip 'n Slide. Bubbles tumble over backyard fences in an afternoon's circuit.

Begin

My daughter has drawn me a picture of how she got up from lunch at daycare, drawn the way she brushed her hair to blue-black lines, and in between, the deep-dark-woods. Once we get home we take an afternoon nap where the kempt nuthatch, the shy pair of cardinals, will work around our sleep. She sucks as if she thinks around her thumb. The day is the day: dozing on a blue chair, a woman. That would be me. Extravagance, any kind of ending. I suspect I'm beginning to lose my interest in ideas.

Tireless

Upstairs I can hear her cough catch, outside it's been snowing for centuries. Snowflakes come from an era of many holes wild to replace themselves. All for *the believing in arriving*, as a friend said. Snow is tireless and so is falling. Buddha watched Teresa cross the gravelly landscape, starting in the evening when the ground cooled enough for her to place her feet on it: toenails ten moons. Buddha absorbed her gait. She got neither closer nor farther away. Centuries dawdle like a thing, and it was not exactly in the way. This winter I would like to tighten my hearing so I can mark the lightning withheld in a flake. I go up and bed sit, put my hand on LiLi's chest, feel her heartbeat. For the nonce, grasses lilting.

Prised

In the evening class I start to take off my coat, stick my hand in the pocket and pull out a toppling handful: dozens of nubs of crayons. Like a surprised heap of marbles but waxed and hued orange, amethyst, aquamarine, pomegranate. I show them to the people next to me, in my fist more color than anywhere in the entire hall. It's night, around the building spins a granular white, snow's dedicated amusia. If you were to sing a song out in that howl it would shave your note to a tight focus, maybe to nothing. If you were to sing harder. At home Li had found my coat and bundled it with the perfect crayon cache, now no one has to be lost. Now flowers can live in the body, colors spill from pockets.

Tag

Forewarned to bring flashlights, our field trip enters the darkened South Haven museum—power out in the whole place. The guide stops near a shadowy display of a lighthouse beacon, tells the kids about a schooner in Lake Michigan, mid-winter a hundred years ago. It was sinking. Calmly the captain directed the crew and passengers to pack their bags, wait on deck, and at the precise moment—lip of ship lowered to ice—gave the word. And they stepped onto floes, walked the way to Chicago. The children sweep flashlight discs, walk on floes of light. To them the story is all too believable. The sleeping curfews, the waking many. Light tag on the ceiling. You're it: a statue. In vacating the schooner, not one soul was lost. Funny how childhood works, making its own missed ways.

Lilac House

We lie on the lawn outside Lilac House B&B on Mackinac Island—three mothers, three daughters, grass cooling our backs, drawing calm from the ground into ourselves, evening coming on. It unfurls the bats, flicking outlines within half-inches around our faces and bodies. Struggling confetti. Pay no attention to claptrap cosmologies, these animals don't make mistakes—no tangling hair, no touch at all, just overall black butterfly fannings. They swipe our breaths. If Buddha could emit flames and waves simultaneously from his body, we can lie here outlined with simple flight. The oldest daughter jumps up, runs to the house, wings framing and reframing her in fluttered profiles, lunge for lunge. She relinquishes them, step by step, they peel off her.

The Ways of Bamboo

On LiLi's dresser-top the bamboo plant braids itself. On the floor pens and books and socks sunder toward each other in looser queues. When she was little we read a story of two girls, Water-Lily and the Dragon King's daughter, who together saved the village by throwing a bundle of bamboo sticks in the torrent: the sticks swelled, tamped the flood to trickle, saved the people. Bamboo's adjustable look, segments pulling light jade from settled jade. The girls grew to be fast friends, like two greens. Growing as water can take body. My daughter is almost my height now. A Chinese emperor, once it was explained to him, said he understood everything about Western civilization except how it progressed without it. When I braid her hair, a reverse braid forms below my fingers.

The Richard Snyder Publication Series

This book is the 19th in a series honoring the memory of Richard Snyder (1925-1986), poet, fiction writer, playwright and longtime professor of English at Ashland University. Snyder served for fifteen years as English Department chair and was co-founder (in 1969) and co-editor of the Ashland Poetry Press. He was also co-founder of the Creative Writing major at the school, one of the first on the undergraduate level in the country. In selecting the manuscript for this book, the editors kept in mind Snyder's tenacious dedication to craftsmanship and thematic integrity.

Deborah Fleming, Series Editor, selected finalists for the 2015 contest.
Final judge: David St. John

Snyder Award Winners:

1997: Wendy Battin for *Little Apocalypse*
1998: David Ray for *Demons in the Diner*
1999: Philip Brady for *Weal*
2000: Jan Lee Ande for *Instructions for Walking on Water*
2001: Corrinne Clegg Hales for *Separate Escapes*
2002: Carol Barrett for *Calling in the Bones*
2003: Vern Rutsala for *The Moment's Equation*
2004: Christine Gelineau for *Remorseless Loyalty*
2005: Benjamin S. Grossberg for *Underwater Lengths in a Single Breath*
2006: Lorna Knowles Blake for *Permanent Address*
2007: Helen Pruitt Wallace for *Shimming the Glass House*
2008: Marc J. Sheehan for *Vengeful Hymns*
2009: Jason Schneiderman for *Striking Surface*
2010: Mary Makofske for *Traction*
2011: Gabriel Spera for *The Rigid Body*
2012: Robin Davidson for *Luminous Other*
2013: J. David Cummings for *Tancho*
2014: Anna George Meek for *The Genome Rhapsodies*
2015: Daneen Wardrop for *Life As* It